971.1 S824h

M

STELTZER
A HAIDA POTLACH

14.95

D1070393

A HAIDA POTLATCH

A HAIDA POTLATCH

Ulli Steltzer

Foreword by Marjorie Halpin

University of Washington Press
Seattle and London

Published in the United States of America by the University of Washington Press, 1984 by arrangement with Douglas & McIntyre Ltd. Vancouver, British Columbia.

Library of Congress Cataloging in Publication Data

Steltzer, Ulli.
    A Haida potlatch.

    Includes bibliographic references.
1. Haida Indians – Rites and ceremonies. 2. Potlatch.
3. Indians of North America – British Columbia – Rites
and ceremonies. I. Title.
E99.H2S74   1984   306′08997   84–50907
ISBN 0-295-96159-7

Design by Sally Bryer Mennell
Printed and bound in Hong Kong

For Leslie, Sara and Benjamin,
Children of the Good People.

FOREWORD

FEASTS AND POTLATCHES *were the Haida roads to greatness more than war. The latter, when not waged to avenge injuries, was simply a means of increasing their power to give the former.*

The potlatch, or giving-away of property, is to be carefully distinguished from the feast of which it might be said to be a "ritualized" form. It was the great event upon which a Haida's social life turned. There were two kinds of potlatches.

The greater, called Wā'ɬgal, was given by a chief to the members of his own clan, on the occasion of a house-raising, adoption of another chief's son, or the tattooing of his friends' children, and the cutting of apertures for labrets, ear-rings, ear-pendants, nose-ornaments, etc.

As a chief borrowed from the opposite clan through his wife, and paid back to the heads of his own clan who were the husbands or wives of those he borrowed of, the potlatch seems to have been an endless chain of property, a large portion of the wealth in the place being massed into a man's hands for the occasion. . . .

The Sî̱ k!ᵃ potlatch was only made at the raising of a grave-post (x̄āt) for a dead chief by the man who took his place, and was given to the members of the opposite clan who had previously attended to the funeral.

Dances of the secret society (literally, "those caused to be inspired") were indispensable accompaniments of a potlatch. . . . The dances of the secret society occurred at every potlatch, and at no other times.

The Haida Secret society was ingrafted upon their shamanistic notions. Just as a shaman was supposed to be inspired by some supernatural being who "spoke," or as they generally preferred to translate it to me, "came through," him, so the Ū́lala [Cannibal] spirit, the Dog-eating spirit, the Grisly-Bear spirit, and so on, "came through" the secret-society novice. I do not know how seriously this possession was taken, but anciently it seems to have been in good faith.

John R. Swanton, 1909: 155–161

As an anthropologist, a professional observer of traditional peoples, I was trained in the 1950s and 1960s to believe that cultural differences were rapidly eroding all over the world. I was taught that processes of ethnic assimilation to the dominant Western technoculture were inevitable and irreversible, and that the mission of anthropology was to record human differences before they disappeared forever.

Now, from the perspective of the 1980s, it is clear that around the middle of the century, a great tide of sentiment on our globe began to turn, and ethnicity — collective human differences — began to be of social value again. In villages and urban ghettos around the world, people who have retained ethnic identity are now asserting it. This is especially true in Canada, which has an official government policy of multiculturalism, under which it encourages and supports the expression of ethnicity among its peoples. An anonymous urban multitude for whom ethnicity is not a matter of personal identity took on the role of watchers or witnesses vis-à-vis this phenomenon.

The role of witness is of special importance to the Haida and other Northwest Coast native peoples. In a potlatch, or ritualized feast, the crucial distinction is the giving of wealth by the hosts to the guests in payment for the latter's witnessing the transfer of honorific names and crests from one generation to the next.

The significance of ancestral names cannot be overemphasized. Haida society can be thought of as an enduring structure of names handed down to successive generations of people who, in their turn, become the ancestors. It is a great responsibility. Ancestral names carried a family's prestige, associated crests and privileges, and rights to economic resources. The potlatch was, and now is again, a public ritual performed in order to bring a new generation into the structure of names. Family and village headmen, or chiefs, are the ones who carry the highest names. Great care must be taken to ensure that the children of noble families merit their high names.

Adoption is the means by which outsiders are brought into a name during their lifetimes. (Adoptees do not pass their names down; the names go back to the family at death.) Adoption extends the privileges and responsibilities of family to others and is considered a great honour.

What a crest is requires some explanation. Let us return to Swanton (1909: 107–108):

> *Each family had the right to use a certain number of crests — i.e., figures of certain animals, certain other natural objects [clouds, moon, etc.], and occasionally articles of human manufacture — during a potlatch; or they might represent them upon their houses or any of their property, and tattoo them upon their bodies. Theoretically the crests used by the Raven families should be absolutely distinct from those used by the Eagles. . . .*

(Haida society is divided into two "sides," the Ravens and the Eagles; membership in a side is inherited from one's mother.) The oldest and most important crest of the Ravens is the Killerwhale, and of the Eagles, the Eagle. Other Raven crests are the Grizzly, Thunderbird, Moon and Flicker. Eagle crests include Frog, Cormorant, Beaver, Sculpin and Wasgo — a Sea Wolf with Killerwhale fins. In this book, the animal designs of people's robes, headdresses, drums and jewellery are crest images.

The traditional forms of Northwest Coast artifacts, especially Haida, are considered by outsiders who know them well to be among the most complex aesthetic forms to be found in any cultural tradition. Even in the old days, mastering these forms required the special training of apprenticeship. Such specialization is rare in aboriginal hunting and fishing (i.e., nonagricultural) societies. The standard anthropolgical explanation for its development on the Northwest Coast is an economic one. Considerably oversimplified, it goes something like this: The abundant natural resources of the coastal environment, most notably salmon, when coupled with techniques for preserving summer foods for consumption in winter, enabled these communities to free certain of their members from full-time participation in the food quest. Some of these people were thus able to devote their time and energy to artistic production. What we must also assume, of course, is that this artistic production, which was sustained over some three thousand years, provided something of great value to the artists' fellow tribespeople.

In modern times, as the Haida made the transition to a Western industrial economy, they gradually abandoned their traditional arts. By the 1920s, their homes, utensils, boats, clothing and so on were indistinguishable from those of the dominant culture. Such carving as was still done was motivated by the tourist market rather than native use. Their continuing differences from non-natives were in the domains of social organization, language and belief rather than in art and ceremony.

The founder of the modern folkcraft movement in Japan, Sōetsu Yanagi, writes about tradition as the accumulation of the experience and wisdom of many generations and calls it the Given Power — a power that transcends the individual craftsman. Confusion about how this works has led to some rather crude misconceptions about so-called primitive art. It is often thought to be the product of blind cultural forces that automatically express themselves through human hands. This is, of course, believed to be the opposite of creative work in the Western tradition.

In truth, Northwest Coast art and many other highly stylized tribal traditions are characterized by extreme variability within certain prescribed constraints. Far from diminishing personal creativity, these constraints bring it forth, require it, compel it. "Once tradition has died out," writes Yanagi (1978: 221), "it is necessary for individual artists to work in place of tradition. Their purpose, however, must not be to work for themselves or by themselves, but to prepare the way to make a new tradition." What we are now witnessing on the Northwest Coast and in this book, I believe, are artists taking up their responsibility to the tradition of their people. They are doing it consciously, deliberately and at considerable personal expense.

Why? The revival of Northwest Coast art in the 1960s and 1970s was clearly stimulated by economic forces, notably a growing tourist demand for souvenirs. Artists of the calibre of Robert and Reggie Davidson, Joe David and Art Thompson have gone far beyond tourist production — their best work is eagerly sought by museums and collectors both in Vancouver and elsewhere. And yet they are producing fine materials, work that could be sold for many thousands of dollars, just to be worn and given away in potlatches and celebrations in native villages. An economic explanation for this phenomenon is insufficient.

I think it has something to do with dancing, and perhaps it also had something to do with dancing three thousand years ago as well. At the turn of the century when the Haida still danced as a matter of course, they told Swanton that people who had not been initiated into the dancing societies had "dark faces" and "stopped up minds." The faces you will see in Ulli Steltzer's fine photographs are, as Joe David says, shining "like the light around the sun." Look closely at these faces and you will see what dancing is about.

In the old days the Haida potlatched to each other — and danced — when a new house was built and when a man raised a totempole in honour of his uncle, whose noble name he inherited and pledged his life to uphold. Today, not only has the occasion for the event changed but so have the witnesses. The Haida are now potlatching as a people to the world. Through Ulli's camera, you and I are invited to be their witnesses.

Marjorie Halpin

Swanton, John R.
    1909   Contributions to the Ethnology of the Haida. New York: American
            Museum of Natural History.
Yanagi, Sōetsu
    1978   The Unknown Craftsman: A Japanese Insight into Beauty. Foreword
            by Shoji Hamada. Adapted by Bernard Leach. Kodansha
            International Ltd. Distributed through Harper & Row, New York.

INTRODUCTION

The invitation to Robert Davidson's potlatch read as follows:

> You are invited to witness the naming of *xa.adaa 7laa git'lang 7isis* (children of the good people) and the adoption of Joe David to the *t'sa.ahl 7laanaas* Tribe. November 6 & 7 1981, George M. Dawson School, Masset, B.C.

Robert and his family had been friends of mine for many years, and Masset had become my second home. Naturally I wanted to contribute to the potlatch, so I asked Robert how he would like me to help. "You could take photographs," said the artist. Two months later, during the second night of the potlatch, I was one of the many people to be handsomely rewarded for their work.

The potlatch with all its different and vital activities lingered in my mind, leaving me with a set of photographs and a lot of questions. So much had been given; so many people had been involved. Almost two years had passed when I asked Robert for an interview and for his permission to publish his thoughts along with the pictures. He kindly agreed. Fortunately video tapes of both nights were made available to me during my visit in Masset, helping me to retrieve some of the speeches. Further interviews with people who had participated in the celebration in one way or another enabled me to gain new insights and so to broaden the material. Thus, the text for this book represents contributions made during the potlatch as well as people's subsequent reflections.

During my interviews I encountered the occasional duplication of terms applied to moieties and clans; both were referred to as tribes. I took the liberty of reserving the word "tribe" for groups of people outside the Haida nation. The moieties Eagle and Raven will be referred to as "sides." Groups of people related through matrilineage will be referred to as "clans." Clans are subdivisions of each moiety.

Some of the Haida names were translated by the people speaking and they are indicated in parentheses or quotation marks. Other Haida words and names have official translations and these appear within square brackets throughout the book.

The word "potlatch" is not a Haida word. It derives from a similar sounding word, used by the people on the west coast of Vancouver Island, meaning "to give." It became part of the Chinook jargon, a trade language, and was soon applied to any ceremonial distribution of property among different coast peoples regardless of the specific nature of the event. The Haida had their own words for their so-called potlatches of the pre-missionary period. People in Masset nowadays like to use the word "doing" for their various feasts and gatherings.

A potlatch may be the creation of one person, but it requires the participation, the help, the goodwill of many others to carry it out. Similarly, this book has been generously contributed to by many people sharing their time and knowledge, their thoughts and feelings with me. May it be a small return for their kindness.

My special thanks go to Florence Davidson who knows how to give, and whose table and wisdom have nourished many generations. I am deeply grateful to John Enrico, linguist and friend. He not only gave me the spelling and translation of Haida names but also, through his knowledge of Haida culture and social structure, protected me from committing major errors. Allan Wilson of Masset graciously lent me his video tapes. Thank you, Allen. My sincere appreciation goes to Marjorie Halpin for making time to write the Foreword to this book.

Bear Mother pole, carved for the people of Masset and raised in 1969 by Robert Davidson.

Robert Davidson

In the past, people lived by a strict code of laws that was defined by public opinion. Since there were no written documents, all changes to the existing order were made at feasts and potlatches, at a time when the public was present. If you accepted the chieftainship, or you raised a memorial pole, or you got married, all activities were recorded this way. So when you decided to change the pattern, you had to accumulate the goods to create the potlatch and invite the people. You paid the people of the opposite side for witnessing the change you made. If a person did not come, or did not accept your gift, that was his way of saying, I don't accept what you are doing. You wanted to invite everybody so they couldn't turn around afterwards to squabble about it.

My knowledge of the proper procedures for the potlatch came from experience, from the time I raised the totempole in the village in 1969. I wanted to do it right, so I knocked on doors and called people together. I said, "I don't know how to do this, I want some help, how do you do it?" People were very co-operative and also very critical because I am Eagle and carving this totempole I should also put an Eagle on top of the pole. But I said, "No, I want the pole to be for everybody; it belongs to the village. I don't want it to be one man's totempole." That was a radical change. The totempole became a focal point, a school, a vehicle for knowledge. For the potlatch it was the same thing, it worked the same way. There are all kinds of experience in name-giving among the elders so I asked them how to proceed. I was very aware that a lot of people could not afford to have a potlatch, so I invited the village to use this for a time to give names.

Robert Davidson

The Haida are divided into moieties — into two sides — the Eagles and the Ravens. Different clans have different crests but everybody is either Eagle or Raven. Masset is predominantly a Raven village because in the past so many women were Raven and had many daughters. I come from the Eagles because my mother was Eagle. My father is Raven — you are supposed to get married to the opposite side.

My seven aunts are Ravens. They have strongly supported me over the years. Nonnie (grandmother) told them, "You've got to help this guy." She has been the main influence in the family. She brought me up, she pushed me to be thoughtful. It seems that I have been chosen to carry the torch.

Florence Edenshaw Davidson with her daughters Virginia, Primrose, Emily, Aggie, Myrtle, Merle and Clara.

Robert Davidson

About a year and a half before the potlatch I said to Joe (David), "I want to adopt you," and he said, "Wow!" Then, about eleven months before the potlatch, at Christmas time, we had a special dinner at which I asked my uncle, Alfred Davidson, to announce the potlatch. By that time Dorothy and I were already accumulating gifts.

2

Dorothy Grant

We went up to Masset four or five times just for planning, to set up
different committees. It seems to work best this way. I was in charge
of the food committee — with Nonnie's supervision of course. With
all her years of experience, she knew just what and how much I
should buy and whom I should ask to help. For one night we
planned to have stew, for the other night traditional food. Uncle
Claude and Sarah were in charge of the stew. Many people were
helping us, making all kinds of different dishes. Winnie Yeltatzie,
who has the biggest kitchen, prides herself on being able to produce
a whole lot of things at once. I asked her to do the pies and she
looked really pleased. She made ninety of them.

Dorothy Grant catches a big red snapper on a food-gathering trip to the
southern Queen Charlotte Islands.

Claude Davidson cleaning abalone.

Florence Davidson

The one who makes the potlatch gets lots of food for it. In the past just his slaves helped him. They picked berries, all kinds of things; they got fish, they dried fish.

4

Floyde Collinson and Norm Bentley digging clams.

While looking for mussels, Dick Wilson spots an octopus.

Floyde Collinson, jigging for cod, catches this eighty-pound halibut instead.

Early in May the people of Skidegate dry their *k'aaw* [herring eggs] on kelp.

Merle Adams whipping the precious soapberries just before the feast.

Florence Davidson

We don't have soapberries on the Island, they bring them to us from the mainland.

Dorothy Grant

Dance practice was going on all over the place, at Nonnie's, Uncle Claude's, Amanda's, Grace's, and we had our own group, the "Urban Haidas" in Vancouver.

Deedee Hageman, Missy Samuels and Leslie Williams Davidson during dance practice at Claude and Sarah Davidson's house.

Dora Brooks

I learned many Indian songs from my mother. When she made baskets she used to sing. She worked and she sang. She was always busy making baskets, and when she went to bed she sang old Gospel hymns. Mother lived over in Alaska for quite a while when she got married to my father. That's why she knew Alaskan songs. After my grandfather died she moved back here to take care of my grandmother.

Some of the songs they dance to, some of them are not for dancing — they are too serious or too sad, or they just don't have the rhythm to dance to. Some of the dances have no words, just chant, I guess. I taught Robert lots of songs. I sang for him on tape because I didn't want to sit there teaching him. He learned all the ones he liked.

Selina Peratrovich, who is ninety-two, listens closely to Robert Davidson's singing. Behind Robert are Dorothy Grant and Emily Gertzen.

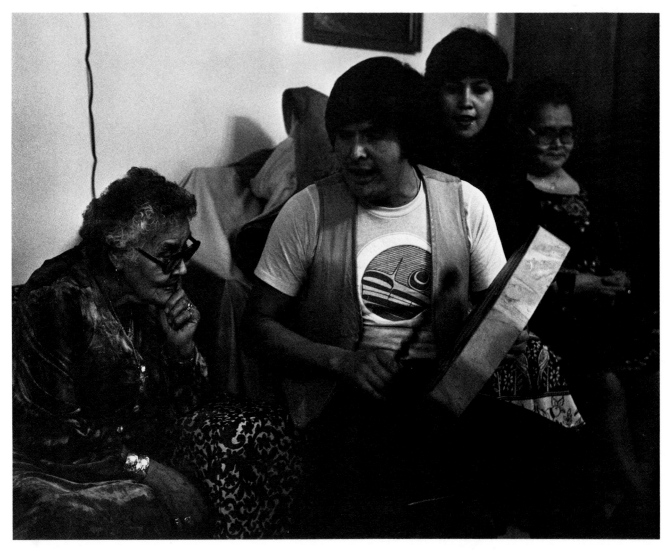

Dorothy Grant

As soon as Robert got the idea of doing the potlatch, he had all his aunties together and he asked them for their support. The Davidsons are an incredibly hardworking family and they worked from the time he told them, right up to the time of the potlatch, producing handmade things. You would see them throughout the year and they would say, "I have so many sweaters made," or, "I have so many crocheted hand cloths, so many aprons made so far." You could just see in your mind all that stuff piling up.

Dorothy Grant finishing off a button blanket for Sara Davidson. This is one of two blankets she made for the potlatch; the other one will be given to Joe David.

Primrose Adams weaving a spruce root hat.

Robert Davidson

The support for your potlatch should come from your side, and it
did, but my main support came from the Ravens — my aunties,
Dorothy and my grandmother — so I had to pay them. You don't
pay your own side; you acknowledge them, but you pay the high-
ranking people of the opposite side.

The night before the potlatch Robert's aunts bring all the presents they have
made to their mother's house, piling them up on long tables and inspecting
each other's handiwork.

Dorothy Grant

Robert, Merle, and I sat down and decided who was going to get
what. I had bought sixty beautiful bath towels. Nonnie wanted those
to go to all the visitors because they had come a long way. The
drums went to the people who were really into dancing and singing,
and also to young kids as an inspiration to them. The drums, I think,
were the most special gifts. Robert worked on them all year long and
hand-painted most of them. Towards the end he gave some to other
people to paint — it was just too much — and he started to carve the
bracelets. Primrose made five spruce root hats and a number of small
baskets. I think she got a gold bracelet for that.

Merle Adams checks long lists of names with careful consideration, while Robert and Dorothy match each name to the appropriate present.

The gold and silver bracelets will be presented in velvet pouches.

Guests from Vancouver Island's west coast help transport the presents from the Haida village to the school in Masset.

The school auditorium is undergoing a transformation. The tables will seat four hundred people comfortably.

THE FIRST NIGHT

Robert Davidson

Inviting people from other tribes to come to your potlatch adds
prestige. It is important to be recognized by outsiders, like people
from Alaska, Bella Bella, Hazelton, Vancouver.

These guests can be recognized easily as coming from K'san by their different blankets, the frog and the
one-horn goat.

Three young visitors from Hydaburg, Alaska.

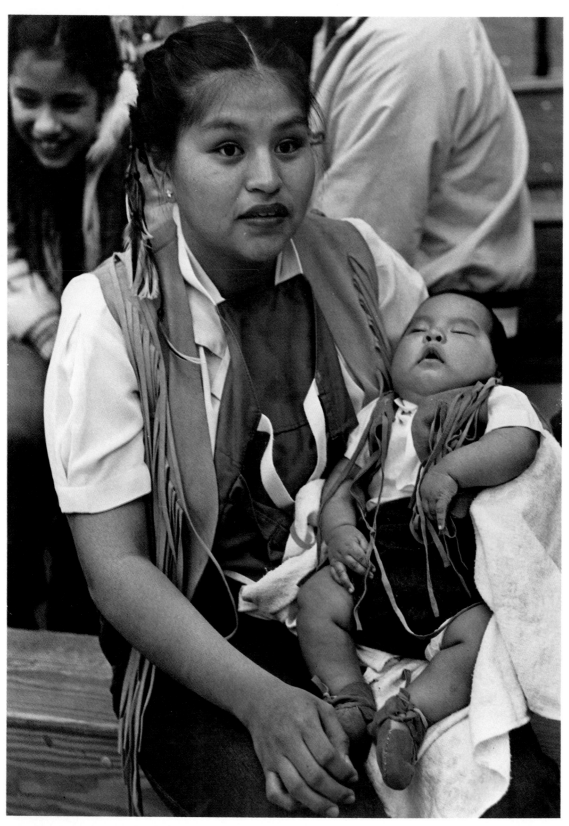

Christal Swanson and her baby, dressed for the dances.

Grace Wilson Dewitt

I gave names to my children and all my grandchildren. This is the first time I announced them in public. It just came natural to do it, just like my weaving when I first started it.

Grace Wilson Dewitt and Emily Abraham in conversation.

The guests are seated, prayer has been offered, and dinner is being served.

Victor Adams

If you have a good master of ceremonies, he is the one that makes it.
Same thing like at a wedding, he has to know a little bit about what
is going on. Most people here don't. I've been master of ceremonies
for quite a few things.

In 1947 I was in Alert Bay. I knew Chief Stephen Cook real well.
He sang me four Indian songs — they were all Haida songs — and he
said Haida songs were known throughout the coast, up north and
way down south. They were sung all over because the Haidas had
the best music. So everybody liked Haida songs, and they bought
the right to sing them.

Victor Adams, master of ceremonies for the first night. The youngest dancer, Derek Stephenson, appears slightly early.

The Haida Canoe Paddle Welcome Song.

Gerry Edenshaw and Reggie Davidson put eagle down on each other's headdresses before the Chief's Welcome Dance.

Florence Davidson in the Spirit Dance.

Florence Davidson

In the old days they kept all the things they used for the dances, all the costumes, in the woods. They called them their treasure. They kept them in hiding just in case somebody came from the outside to fight them.

28

Joe David

Change is inevitable, and change is important. Sometimes you get that uncomfortable feeling that you can't change anything. There is always somebody around saying you have to do things the old way; the old ceremonies are dying, you have to hang on, you have to be traditional. The fact is, there is always change and our people have always been comfortable with it. Change is important when you have to make do with what you have.

For example, now some of our ceremonies are getting shorter. Not all of the old people can sit around any more for days on end to listen to someone lay out a history, and to watch the performance of his dances and privileges. Now people come from miles around in cars and at the end of the ceremonies they have to drive again.

Joe David approaches Robert Davidson, accompanied by family wolves.

Robert Davidson

What motivated me to give this potlatch is my concern, my awareness of where we come from and where we are going; my awareness of what can be changed and improved. If I lived in a white man's world I would become a teacher, but I was given the privilege of this knowledge which is not taught in schools or anywhere else. So I feel it is my responsibility to give away what I have — knowledge, experience. I can only do it in the way I was taught. The potlatch is our way of transferring cultural knowledge. If you talk this way and you act this way, this action and talking comes from way back, and when you do it you are giving the knowledge away.

Robert Davidson

By being adopted, Joe is entitled to all the rights of a Haida. At the same time he is obligated to contribute to some of the doings in Masset. When he is ready he will have to give a potlatch in his own village to announce his new rights. I will be there to support him and we will demonstrate the songs and dances he is entitled to use. We, in turn, are entitled to use his songs. We can now do the Wolf Dance, for example. That's what I love about this, it expands our boundaries.

Robert adopts Joe to be his brother.

By exchanging blankets they seal their new relationship publicly.

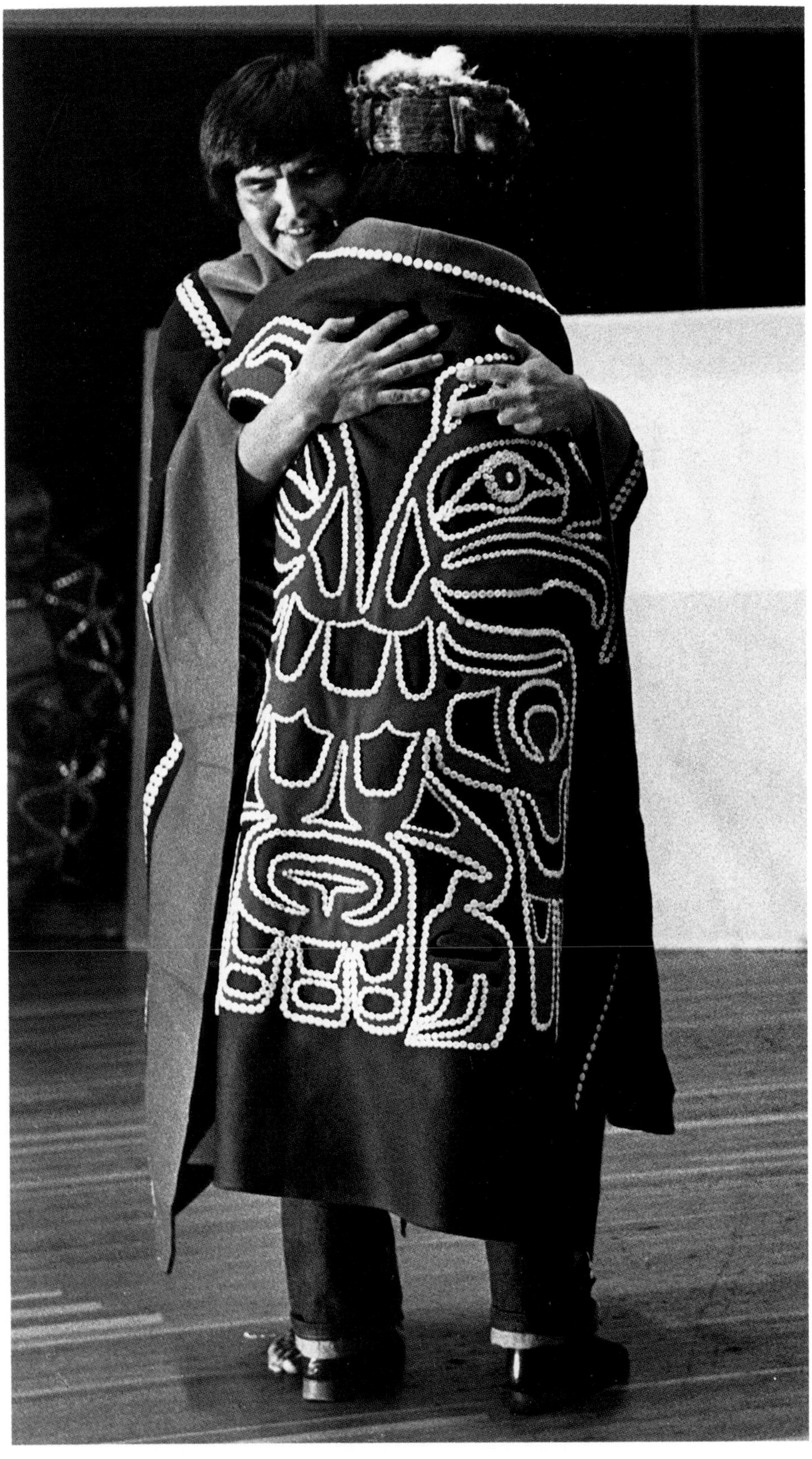

Using his talking stick, Robert announces the adoption of Joe into his clan.

Robert Davidson

haw 7aa, haw 7aa! *Thank you, thank you! Tonight we have adopted into the* t'sa.ahl 7laanaas *clan Joe David. He will be a great contribution to us. Joe has been instrumental in my understanding of Haida culture and history, in my coming back to my roots, because he is so very close to his own tradition. Where he comes from, in his village on the west coast of Vancouver Island, the traditional way of life is still very strong. Joe has helped me in many situations. Several times he supported me through songs when I really needed it. Joe, I give you my crest, the two-headed Eagle!* haw 7aa!

Art Thompson, Joe's nephew from Nitinat Lake, makes a spontaneous speech. Joe's brother George is standing by.

Art Thompson

We are not giving him to you, we are sharing him with you. You can only have half of him!

Joe's family responds to the adoption with songs.

Robert Davidson

Names have to be transferred publicly. The names that are given to us and to our children are ancient names. It was a challenge to the elders to remember the names, and even those who had given away names privately had to question their own right to give them away.

Since the whole village was invited to give names, I thought the Ravens should have first chance, and, since Joe was the focal point, he should get his name on the second day.

Florence Davidson

(This is Florence Davidson's own translation of her speech which she made in the Haida language.)

*I thank you people from far away for coming to my grandson's doing —
Vancouver, Vancouver Island, Hydaburg, Ketchikan, Skidegate, Hazelton.
I thank you very much for coming while it costs so much to travel. My
grandson has been sensible ever since he was a young boy, and his brother is
the same. They don't run around. They have respect for themselves and for
their elders. I am proud of that.*

*Ever since their mother died I made up my mind to be their mother. While
I am their grandmother I treat them like my own sons. That's why they love
me so much too. I really enjoy having grandsons like that.*

Reggie's name is skil kaat'la.aas *[wealth spirit who has arrived] that was
one of his chinny's (grandfather's) names and he gave it to him. Their name
comes from Reggie's great-great-uncle who was the first ordained minister in
Hydaburg.*

*Robert's great-great-uncle in Alaska raised a pole that was the tallest
totempole ever made. It had the two-headed Eagle on top, Robert's crest. It
was called* 7iit'laàgiidgwii kint'ahl — *"looking at all the chiefs from way
up." ("Looking down on all the chiefs" is how we say it in Haida, but
when you say it in English it sounds awful!) That's what my husband's
name was. He was Robert's chinny. Robert's mother was a relative to him
— they were of the same clan. His chinny gave Robert his first name,* guud
saandlaans — *"Eagle on whom it is dawning." I give Robert that name*
7iit'laàgiidgwii kint'ahl.

My sister's name was sgaann jaadgu saandlaans *[killerwhale woman on
whom it is dawning]. I give that name to Sara. Her first name is* skil jadee
[wealth spirit woman].

Benjamin's name is tlajang nang kingaas — *"the one who is known far
away."*

Florence Davidson announces the Haida names of her grandsons, Robert and Reggie Davidson, and of her great-grandchildren, Sara and Benjamin Davidson.

Susan Davidson

I am nan stlaay tuwaa kwiìuwaas [precious greasy hands]. I am the mother of two Haida children, and I am proud to be here with you now. When I hear different speakers say, tonight, the Haida people have only their culture and their heritage, I want to say that the Haida people have their children. I am proud to be part of this Haida family that comes together now to celebrate all of their children. We are here to remember the strength and the sharing of our family and we do it for ourselves and for our children.
     Thank you!

Susan Davidson with her children, Sara and Benjamin.

Ida Smith

When my kids were small — there was Mary, Robert, Pete and Irene — their grandfather named them; he gave them Indian names. But Emily Abraham says that the name he gave to Irene belongs to her, so last minute we switched it. This is kind of new to us, all these names given to our children in public. In my growing life I never saw that. But that's the way Robert wanted it.

I used to go with a guy from Skidegate when we were living down there. He was Raven. Well, I am Raven too. My mother used to bother me and say, "He's your brother." I said, "Jee, nothing but brothers around. What are we going to do, marry a white man?" I wasn't allowed to go with him. In the old days, if you are Raven and you marry a Raven they don't have respect for your children. That's why my mother didn't want me to go around with this guy, and we had to listen to our parents.

Ethel Jones

I should have married someone from the opposite side, Eagle. I am Raven and Pete was Raven. I think we were the first to do it that way.

Florence Davidson

My father was given ten names to ensure his position in the village. When he was born they called him Tahayghen. The last name they gave him was *nang kwiigee tlaa.ahls* [one who is tenfold precious]. Every time they gave him a name, they tattooed him. My dad had tatoos on his back and his front and his arms and his hands, right down to his ankles, Haida design, the same way as they do now on prints.

When my father got married the minister, Mr. Harrison, wanted to call him Charles Tahayghen, but Albert Edward Edenshaw, his uncle, said, "No! His name is going to be Edenshaw. He is going to be the next chief." So Mr. Harrison put down Charles Edenshaw. They made my mother sign the book in church. They called her Isabella Edenshaw. "I don't want Eagle's name," she says. "I can't take Eagle's name; I am Raven." They kept on explaining; finally she understood it.

Ida Smith announces the Haida names of her daughter, Irene Pollard, and of her granddaughter, Susan Smith.

Ida Smith

I thank you all, and I thank Robert Davidson, for he is way younger than us and yet we are learning from him. I appreciate his way, and what he is doing for us.

I give my daughter Irene the name jaad 7iljuus *[high ranking woman], after my mother. To my granddaugher Susan I give the name* jaasanaas *[no translation known], after my mother's sister. Thank you!*

Susan Smith

I was excited to get a Haida name, but I wished I knew the meaning of it.

Ethel Jones

My mother had long given up having children when I came along. That's why people were happy when I was born and gave me names. Emily Abraham's mother gave me the name *haayganiig* [no translation known]. It is a Raven name, but it belongs to her clan, not to my clan. I can't pass it on; it will go back to their clan when I leave this earth.

Some people call me *k'amii*. It is more or less a pet name. It is hard for me translate that one; it means "precious," and it means "glass."

I was born in 1920. In 1930 the boarding schools (Indian residential schools) were introduced to the coast. And even though there were just three of us, my parents sent us to St. Michael's School at Alert Bay. They couldn't stand being separated from us so they moved down to Alert Bay for one whole year.

When we first got to the school, we didn't even know when to use the word "yes" and when to use the word "no." We had never spoken a word of English. That is such a short time ago and in those few years we have almost lost our language. I did not teach my children Haida; we thought that learning English was the most important thing in life, because everything went that way.

Adolphus Marks

In 1778 the first white man stepped on these Islands, that was at *k'yuust'aa,* northwest from here, that's where my people come from. Before that time everyone had Indian names. Today so many names are forgotten. You can't blame the new generation, it's their parents' fault that they were not told. Today they say that the young generation is dumb. They are not dumb. It's the old people's fault that they didn't teach their children, speak Haida to them.

Adolphus Collinson

When the missionaries came to us they said, "You don't worship those totempoles, you worship God!" And they told us to cut them down. Charlie Gladstone was a boat builder and he had a dandy pole standing beside his big boathouse. He paid me twenty dollars to cut it down. At that time that was a lot of money. We had no chainsaw then, just a saw. There was another guy with me. It's so long ago, I can't even remember his name. The two of us cut down that pole, it didn't take any time. We cut it in blocks for firewood.

Ethel Jones announces the Haida names of her nephew, Frank Parnell, her daughter, Jocelyn Allen, and her son, Alex Jones.

Ethel Jones

If we don't keep up our tradition in this generation, the next one will know less, it will all be gone. By letting us give Haida names to our children and grandchildren, Robert is keeping our minds open to our past. We need that. Our Haida names were slipping away from us, they were almost forgotten in our village.

To Frank Parnell I want to give the name 7unskaagang [carrying a small object on back]. To Jocelyn I give the name jaadgu saandlaans [woman on whom it is dawning]. Alex Jones, my son, I give him the name gyaawhlans [no translation known].

Thank you very much. haw 7aa!

Alex Jones

Some of our boys are working right now on a map of the north end of the Island, and they are getting all the old Indian names recorded on that map — places where the Haidas used to stop off, make tents, where they used to rest.

I'm glad it is all starting to come back to the village. I got a Haida name, but I don't know the history of names. That potlatch Robert put on was my first experience with names. See, I wasn't really interested, but now I think he did something that is important to people because they started questioning each other. They all knew about names before, but they were afraid to come out and talk. Now they are not afraid to come out and talk. Before they were tense, now they are starting to be relaxed when they are talking about their Haida history. Robert knew the potlatch was going to cost him an arm and a leg, but he had enough courage to put it on. I believe he knew that he was going to get it back, but it took a lot of courage to do it.

Forrest Dewitt

The Raven dance is to make the people happy; it is a Tlingit dance. Our dances are close to Haida dances. The older people in Masset can understand them — not the language but the action, the movements.

I was born in Alaska. My mother died when I was four years old, so I was raised by my father's old uncles. That's where I learned quite a bit about our Tlingit culture. When I came to be a teenager, church people and pastors put a stop to it all. That is against God, what you Tlingits are doing, Indian dance. And they tell us to burn up the totempoles. So there was no Indian dance for a long, long time. The kids were not allowed to speak Tlingit at school, not even in the school yard when they were playing for ten or fifteen minutes at recess. If the teachers caught you speaking Tlingit to your friends, you got punished for it. So the language was lost altogether.

Much later we find out that our culture is not against God, it's not against the law. So we try to get it back, teach the younger people. But it is hard to get the language back. We are teaching them, but it is hard for them to learn.

At the end of the first night Forrest Dewitt, Tlingit from Ketchikan, Alaska, dances the Raven Dance.

THE SECOND NIGHT

Jerry Williams

I was just given a piece of paper and told, "You do this." I don't know why I was picked. They just said, "We'd like you to be master of ceremonies. This is how it is to go. If you want to make changes let us know and we'll get together." I just do what I'm told.

My mom and dad never spoke Haida in front of us. If you don't learn Haida or any of the cultural things, now that the culture is starting to come back it is difficult to get interested in it. I support Claude's dancing group because I have a daughter in there and I think he is doing a good job with the kids.

Sara Davidson
(age ten)

I danced at the potlatch and got many pictures taken. In one of them I have a funny face. My Chinny Claude got real mad at me, I mean *real* mad. He is such a strict Haida, he wants everything perfect. You get so bored. You have practised all this time and then there are all these spotlights on you and all these people watching you, no wonder you make a funny face.

Claude Davidson dancing a bear hunting song.

K'san dancers, Hal Blackwater from Kispiox, and Sadie Mowatt from Hazelton, in an ancient spirit dance.

The audience responds to the spirit dance.

Lak Nok Dance (one-horn goat dance), by K'san dancers.

K'san dancers returning a Haida song.

Doreen Jensen

We, the people of K'san, would like to thank Robert and his village of Haida for the invitation to join this happy gathering, the naming of the children of Haida.

It is a great honour for us to be able to lend support to Robert at this time. Early in our organization he was one of the people who came to help us when we needed someone to guide us in the revival of our art. Robert was a young man of twenty-three at the time, and he contributed a great deal to the success of our project. In the naming ceremony tonight Robert is challenging the young people of Haida to contribute to the revival of their own heritage.

Long ago, people from different villages and nations gave each other songs, crests and dances as a token of respect. Tonight we have the privilege of bringing back a Haida song. This song was given to us many years ago. We call it limx luu am a goot, which means "song for a happy heart." Tonight we have happy hearts because we are bringing it back. On this great day when everybody has a happy heart we are using it as a feasting song so that we can give you our soapberries.

Doreen Jensen speaking on behalf of the K'san people.

Adolphus Marks

I tell you something about the Haidas here. Not too long ago we were self-supporting people. We built our own boats, and houses. We used to move five times in one year. Start February, we move to Tow Hill to get clams; there was a cannery there. April, we come here, fix our boats and go to North Island summer camp; stay there till about September. Move here for a while to store our winter food away and then go to one of the rivers where the fish is. It is just a few years back that everything was introduced to us, like welfare, family allowance and things like that. Before that everybody used to help one another. If something went on, you didn't even have to ask for help, everybody knew just what to do. That's the world we were brought up in on this Island. Love one another and help one another. The whole village was like one family.

The old people used to see things; they knew the world was going to be like it is today. Nobody will listen to each other any more, they predicted that a long time ago.

Potlatch time, that's talking many many years ago. Even some of the old people living today don't know too much about it. The preachers at that time thought different of what our people should do, you see. They thought people were praying to the totempole, while it was just clans showing their crests, like Raven, Eagle, Killerwhale, Bear, all that. That totempole was telling a story, that's why it was standing there.

He is a thinking man now, that Robert. To start things like that is quite something! He's been travelling, he's been away, he's learned quite a bit. If you stay around here today, you see nothing, you learn nothing. I am glad to see them do the potlatch today. It is something the new generation should learn. It makes them happy. They will never do it the way it was, but they are giving it a try.

Some people have been giving names all along, but this was the first time in a while that names were given in public. A lot of people gave their nieces and nephews names at their house, but it wasn't done in public. It is very important that it be done in public so that everybody will know.

Adolphus Marks

Robert has adopted a brother from Nootka last night, tonight he is giving him a Haida name. His name is going to be skil k̲'aahluus [wealth spirit arising].

Joe is lucky to get into a good size family like the Davidsons are. He can fish at any of their places at any time. Joe comes from a different place, and they are doing things differently everywhere. But Robert will teach him how to do things around here. Joe has to come here again.

Joe, I welcome you!

Adolphus Marks, the oldest person of Robert's clan, gives a Haida name to Joe. Amanda Edgars, Dora Brooks and Arlene Nelson, members of the same clan, stand by to support the transaction.

Joe David

Thank you, Haida Nation, brothers and sisters; thank you each and every one tonight. Thank you, who have come a long way; thank you, who did so much to make sure that these people were taken care of. They were fed properly and cared for properly.

Thank you very much for taking me into your hearts. I have been coming here for three or four years; right from the start I was welcome. I was taken into families, I was made a friend of many — Skidegate, Masset, Hydaburg. You all did a great deal for me. Everywhere I go, and at home, I will speak of the love and praise I feel for you people.

The west coast people respond to the naming of Joe with Welcome Mask songs.

Joe David

At home, on the west coast of Vancouver Island, all the families still know their songs and practise these songs and form a unit of singers among themselves to present these songs. They never use songs from outside their own family; to do so is considered a shame and is not acceptable. That is why potlatches are given, so the records are kept straight. People will stand and recite exactly where that name and that song comes from and how come they have the right to use it. Everyone present, because they are present and paid as witnesses, is to remember that and remember it correctly.

At some point I will give a traditional potlatch. I will bring Robert to my people. They should witness what I got, my name, the songs, the dances. They have to see Robert and the Haida people; they've got to hear Robert sing. I will demonstrate the ownership and privilege, demonstrate the knowledge.

What is wealth but knowledge. You know this song, you know this name, you know the history of this family, their songs and dances. Knowing these things and knowing how to do them is your identity. So you demonstrate your knowledge and you share it, and you share the wealth that goes with it — the beauty of the song and dance and the feasting. It's the feeling of power and life, the energy and the love that Robert is sharing with me, that is around me like the light around the sun, and me bringing it to my people and shining in front of them, to give them that knowledge, that love, that energy — that's what it is all about.

When you pray and prepare, bathe and humble yourself, when you are forging yourself to conduct the energy and strength these songs and dances took to be created, then all those things will come through you to the people. When you are at the potlatch and you feel the song is just right, and the dancer is doing it just right, and everybody is right into it, and they are focussed on it, they can't take their eyes off it, and their heart just swells, and you find it in your throat, and you know that you could close your eyes and still feel it — that's what you are there to do, to share that feeling with the people. To strive for that harmony and unity is how you learn to be a correct human being.

Joe David

My family will sing a song of thanks. The song belongs to our family, the Thompson family, Nitinat, and the David family, Clayoquot. We've been singing two nights now. We are singing in appreciation, we are singing with joy. You fill our hearts, you magnify our spirits and our voices. Everybody here contributes to what is happening. Every single spirit in here is an important part of it. This is not the beginning and it is nowhere near the end. It has been going on for a long time, and it will continue.

Dora Brooks giving Haida names to her nephews. Jerry Williams, holding the microphone for Dora, is master of ceremonies for the second night of the potlatch.

Dora Brooks

I was asked to give names to the children. They didn't have any names yet; their mothers do, but not the young ones.

When I was a child people used to call each other by their Haida names. Not any more. They quit long ago giving names in public, just sometimes they do it at feasts or memorials.

Jerry Williams

There are some things worth preserving. I'd like to see the whole Island preserved. I would hate to look across the Inlet some day and see no tree at all. I sometimes think that the logging companies are speeding up logging because we are getting serious about land claims. They are cleaning everything off before the government even starts to negotiate, before there is a moratorium. By the time everything is settled there will be nothing left on the Island for anybody. When they finally get all the trees off and wreck all the streams where the salmon go they'll say, "Okay, you guys, have your Island back. See how good we are to you? You wanted it back all this time, now you can have it."

It's time for us to shape up. It will do us no good if we don't move along with the white man's culture; if we just hang on to our past. We'll be stuck right where we are and the white man will say, "Look at all the Indians dancing; that's all they are good for. They just stay the way they were when we first ran into them."

But I admire Robert for giving some of the culture back to the village. Some of the people had never heard of a potlatch, didn't know what it was. They saw it there — maybe not exacly the way it was in the past, but that doesn't matter — all those people giving away names to the younger kids, and Robert giving away everything he had!

Dempsey Collinson
(Chief Skidegate)

I want to say that I am proud of Robert's achievements; I am proud and happy to see a young person like him being so dedicated to our Haida heritage. Not only does he have the feeling for our culture in himself, but he also acts and lives it. That is why I am so proud of Robert. I feel towards him like I feel towards my own son. Thank you, Robert. Also, I am very happy to welcome Joe into the Haida nation. He has contributed to our feasts, he has sung for us many times. I am glad to see that Robert took him to be his brother, I am glad he will come back to our beautiful Islands. Welcome, Joe!

Robert Davidson

When I listened to the old people talk — we ought to do this and we ought to do that — I decided to do something about it. So I invited the people: here is this time to give names to your children and to your grandchildren. Some of them flatly refused: "No, we've got to forget the old ways and move on, we are not going to do this." But those two nights they were lining up to name their children.

Carrie Weir giving Haida names to her daughter-in-law, Agatha Weir, and to six of her grandchildren.

Florence Davidson

My husband's father was Chief *naàhlaang*: David *naàhlaang*. When they start going to school they call my husband Robert *naàhlaang*. The minister could not pronounce it, so, because the father was David *naàhlaang* they changed the name by his first name. That's why we are Davidsons.

Daniel was the oldest in the family. They named him in Alaska. He got married to an Alaskan, his uncle's daughter. They call him Nathan over there because they can't say *naàhlaang*: Daniel Nathan.

Moses Ingram giving Haida names to his son, Francis Ingram, and his family.

When I gave names to the boys during another doing at the opening of the hall I looked back to when Roger Weir was the chief, from way out Tow Hill, the village they called Yaagan. That was long time ago. After he died his nephew, Peter Hill, took over. If the chief of a village dies and he has nephews big enough to take over, it gets turned over to them. That's the law. After Peter Hill died, me and Ethel Jones found one to take his place — Alex Jones, Chief *gyaawhlans* [no translation known]. The people from that village were called *kunn 7laanaas*. They are Raven.

At Robert's doing I gave names to my sister's kids and my older son's kids, to my sons and to their wives. My sons got Raven names from their mother's side. The names I gave to their wives and children come from my mother and my grandmother from my side, Eagle.

Francis Ingram, my oldest son, is *kil sdang7waas* [Kil–voice or speech; no translation known]. The mother, Janice Ingram, I gave her the name *xahlkuljuud* [shiny objects laying all over the ground]. The younger boy, Roger Ingram, I gave the name *haanagee* [handsome]. Donald Ingram, the older boy, I gave the name *7anawaad* [no translation known]. That's my name, but that name doesn't belong to me. I was named after my grandfather and I don't own the name but I can give it to my grandson. I gave it back to them because that's their clan's name, so it has to go back to them. They let me use it for a while but it does not belong to my clan. My real name is *gid kagans* [chief's son who escaped destruction]. That name belongs to our clan. The clans have their own names a million years ago and we still use them.

Chief *naàhlaang* [no translation known] from Yaan, across the Inlet, was a different clan from mine. They call that clan *st'langng 7laanaas*. They are Raven. After Chief *naàhlaang* died, my grandfather Jimmy Jones took over. He was Chief *skil kwiit'laas* [skil–wealth spirit; kwiit'laas–no translation known]. After he died, well, Joe Edgar took over. He was my brother-in-law, married to my sister. His Haida name was *naàhlaang*. That name comes back again, Chief *naàhlaang*. After he died, it was turned over to Peter Jones, Ethel Jones's husband. I think his Haida name was Chief *skil 7iw7waans* [big wealth spirit]. After he died Ethel and I found one to take his place, his nephew Edwin Williams. When we took him as chief from Yaan, I gave him that Haida name again, *naàhlaang*.

Reggie Davidson in the Eagle Dance *juu-s-guud-jahlii xi-kaw-yaan-daal* [gliding right along the running tide].

Reggie Davidson

The first Eagle headdress I carved didn't fit on anybody's head. It wasn't until I learned to dance that I understood the art. Next time I did an Eagle headpiece it had a purpose; it could fit on a person's head and be used for dancing. It wasn't heavy like the first one, either. You can get a headache if you dance with all that weight on your head.

There are no old male dancers in Masset anymore; it's just women who are left. So when I started to dance I had to make it up, just try to imitate the animals I was portraying. At first they didn't tell me much more than what I was doing wrong. There was Nonnie and a couple of older people sitting around when we had dance practice. "You just don't dance like women do with their hands on their hips; men don't have their hands on their hips." That's what they said, and they bawled me out. Later, when we danced and we were doing it right — I guess it took them a while to remember — they said, "That's how it is, you do it that way!"

Dancing sure takes a lot of work; you have to practise all the time, and you have to accept criticism, you have to listen and let them show you how it should be done.

We are adding new dances all the time, using the old songs. Robert even composed a new song in English. If they accept it in Masset, well, then it's all right. Some critics say it wasn't done that way, but who is around to tell you how it was done. It is better to do something that we can all relate to and understand. We just go by the little knowledge people gave us and make up the rest. You can tell, when you are doing a new or different dance, whether it works or not. It is like getting in the car and driving: you can drive if you don't hit anything, but if you start hitting things, it doesn't work.

The Dogfish Dance. This was given to the people of Masset by the people of Hydaburg, Alaska, at the occasion of the "Tribute to the Living Haida" in March 1980.

Dorothy Grant

Innovation is important. I see tradition as a continuous process. While we are alive and have still got years and years ahead of us, and will have grandchildren behind us, what are we going to leave them? A few little bits and pieces of what the anthropologists wrote down? We've got the ability to see where our people are at. Why shouldn't we create new things? We seem to get stuck with that word "tradition." Who is to define what tradition is? People say, "Oh, that's not traditional." So what is tradition? Is it something that has a lid on it, and nothing else can be put into that bucket?

When we do a new dance, there is always a risk in that. It is like learning to walk when you are a baby; you have no confidence yet. That only comes with experience, with getting out there and doing it. Dancing is an expression of ourselves. Maybe we just know by instinct how to do it, by the feeling of our heart. Maybe what we are doing now is what our people did long ago.

66

Reggie Davidson in the Paddle Exit Song.

The first drums go to Robert's children, Sara and Benjamin, and to his niece, Leslie.

Leslie Williams Davidson
(age nine)

When I was in kindergarten I learned to drum. My nonnies taught me how, my Nonnie Ethel and my Nonnie Grace. When I was six I also learned to sing Indian songs. My Nonnie Nina is teaching us Haida. When she says some stuff she asks us to say it.

You need a lot of practice when you drum because you have to get into the same beat as your older drummers; you have to get into the same beat as your song.

I never knew I was going to get a drum from Robert, he never told me about it. I was happy when I got it. I guess he must have seen me drum a lot on my school drum. That one was not so nice, it did not have a design on it. My new drum has a sea monster.

Benjamin Davidson
(age seven)

Nonnie announced my name to all the people. They should know! And Robert gave me a drum. There is a Raven on it. Robert painted it and he made the drum. I think that Robert is nice.

Sara Davidson

I like the part of the potlatch when they give out the gifts. You watch them dance and you already know all those dances, that's not so exciting. But I like to get new things, clothes. I've gotten gifts at other times, and there was dancing too, but I've been only to one real potlatch, my dad's potlatch. I got a really pretty coat hanger and all this good food and cakes and stuff, and I got a drum with a dogfish on it. My dad painted it.

Ethel Jones

I was given a drum at the potlatch. Robert made it for me. I use it a
lot when I teach the Haida language and Haida dances in school.
That is a gift that will last for life.

When you get a new blanket, you dance. When you get a new drum, you want to sing.

Robert gives away the precious spruce root hats.

Emma Matthews thanks Robert for her gift.

Members of Robert's family get ready to distribute the smaller gifts.

Merle Anderson and Arlene Nelson, handing out presents.

Florence Davidson

Before my time they collect things for years and years to make potlatch. They get Hudson's Bay blankets in bundles and give them out, sometimes five or ten. They give them to the other side: Ravens give them to Eagles, Eagles give them to Ravens. Robert gave ten sweaters to my side; they all went to the Ravens.

They always have small gifts for everybody: kerchiefs, socks, nylons. The big gifts go to the older ones, to respected people. Robert gave away so many drums too. All the aunties made potholders, aprons and face towels. They cut up big towels and crocheted around them and gave them to him. That's why he gave them bracelets.

Aggie Davis and her daughter, Helen, handing out presents.

Dorothy and the aunties receive their bracelets.

Benjamin watches his father make a speech.

Joe David gives out Robert's print, "Children of the Good People."

Robert Davidson

For the last two nights we have celebrated our forefathers, and we have celebrated the future by giving names to our children. The design you see behind me symbolizes the circle of children, the continuous cycle that we all are part of. Joe will now give out a print that commemorates this event: the circle of children, Eagle and Raven in the centre, xa-adaa 7laa git'lang 7isis, "Children of the Good People."

Robert Davidson

At the potlatch you clean house and give gifts to all the people you feel indebted to from the past. You clean house and you have a fresh start. Some things were forgotten — that leaves room for another potlatch.

We were broke after it was all over, but the return comes hundredfold, as they say. Spiritually I feel rich — rich to have experienced it. You open a door and there are ten more doors, and you open them and there are new ideas for new directions.

Robert and Dorothy give thanks. *haw 7aa! haw 7aa!*